Do You Believe In Growth?

Why Russia & China Keep Rising While US Society Stifles Innovation

A Message From

The Center for Political Innovation

TABLE OF CONTENTS

INTRODUCTION

Growth is good. This should be common sense. It is completely healthy and normal to want to see things improve in your life. It is completely healthy and normal to want a more comfortable life, to provide better for your family, to see things in your community get better, and to take pride in your achievements.

Growth isn't just about money. Sure, seeing a rise in your income is great, but growth is about much more than that. Human beings are tool-making creatures. While other species merely interact with our environment, we force the environment to serve us. The whole history of humanity is a story of constantly reinventing our relationship with nature and reaching a higher plane. Ants have been making their ant farms the same way for thousands of years. Beavers have been making their beaver dams the same way for thousands of years. But in just 7 or 8 thousand years, human beings have gone from hunter-gatherers in the woods to space travel, iPhones, and artificial intelligence.

Humanity is a creative species, constantly striving to expand its population, lengthen its life expectancy, and make living conditions more comfortable. Growth defines humanity.

So, why does it seem like a contrary message is being blasted everywhere? Why does despair, hopelessness, and pessimism seem to be seething throughout Western civilization? Why is "degrowth" suddenly trendy? What has gone wrong?

There's one section of the world where growth is everywhere. UN Secretary-General Antonio Guterres remarked: "Every time I visit China, I am stunned by the speed of change and progress. You have created one of the most dynamic economies in the world while helping more than 800 million people lift themselves out of poverty – the greatest anti-poverty achievement in history."

Since 1949, 850 million people have been lifted from poverty. 70% of the world's poverty reduction has been achieved by the Communist Party of China. China has high-speed trains that can go over 200 miles an hour. China continues to send spacecraft to the far side of the moon to retrieve samples used in fusion energy research, paving the way to a higher energy source than fossil fuels. China is centralizing its Fusion Energy Research with the goal of creating the industrial prototype fusion reactor, or "artificial sun," by 2035.

But China is not alone. Despite devastating sanctions and attempts to isolate the country, the IMF admits that Russia's economic growth continues to expand. Oil exports have held steady, and the state is using oil revenue to expand the industrial base. Russia is experiencing an agricultural boom, now the leading exporter of wheat. Russia responded to sanctions imposed in 2014 by rebuilding its farming system. *The Economist* proclaimed in 2018, "Russia has become an agricultural powerhouse." The growth continues. "By 2030, the production of Russia's agriculture sector is expected to increase by at least one quarter compared to 2021, while exports should rise by half," the Russian President recently explained. Russia is also supplying fertilizer to African countries.

The explosion of growth happening in Russia and China is going global. In October 2023, a publication from Boston University described China's global infrastructure projects: "Go big or go home. That seems to have been the mantra of China's decade-long effort to finance infrastructure projects around the world: an airport in Pakistan, a high-speed train line in Indonesia, a port in Ethiopia, Africa's longest suspension bridge in Mozambique." The article went on to explain: "Between 2013 and 2021, China provided at least $331 billion in financing to an array of countries, largely in the Global South; African countries alone have received $91 billion." The Center for Strategic and International Studies described Russia's expanding economic relationship with Africa: "Trade revenue between Russia and African countries almost doubled from $9.9 billion in 2013 to $17.7 billion by 2021. Grain exports are of particular importance, as nearly 30 percent of Africa's grain supplies come from Russia. Moscow's leading trade partners in the region are countries in North Africa—particularly Egypt, Algeria, and Morocco—which together account for approximately 67 percent of Russia's total trade with the continent. Moscow mainly exports wheat, coal, refined petroleum, and electronics to these states, while importing fruits, sugar, and vegetables.

Asle Toje of the Norwegian Nobel Institute contrasted the pessimism and confusion rising in the West with the explosion of growth and optimism happening in the East: "In the West, the current times are often seen as a time of uncertainty and fears…this agonizing over the future, and we often forget that for many others, especially on the Eurasian continent, this is a golden era, and in the Eurasian continent, we're seeing a lot of power accumulating, we're seeing roads, cities, train networks snaking through the post-Soviet wilderness, and creating a fabulous amount of wealth and dynamism. And this is also happening globally; we are living through a time of great technological progress, a time of engineering marvels that have been unsurpassed in human history."

This short booklet will help you understand the problem and what can be done about it.

Over the past decade, the rise of a certain pessimistic worldview commonly called "woke" has become hard to ignore.

Lets Talk About "Woke"

There is a group of very obnoxious people in society these days, and many of us find them very annoying.

They always want to remind you of how "good" they are. Whatever the latest trendy social media cause is—whether it's #BlackLivesMatter, #StopTrump, abortion, transgender rights—you can be sure they are all over it. While these issues might genuinely matter to them individually, at the widespread level we're talking about, the primary driving factor is being good, correct, and beating everyone else.

And so, they really want *you* to be "wrong." They hope to discover that you are somehow a "bad" person. Talking to them is frightening because they listen to every word you say, hoping to "correct" you and thus prove themselves to be "better."

In their minds, being a "good" person means constantly "exposing," "denouncing," and "disavowing" others. The more they "call out" others, the better they feel.

But their obnoxious traits go beyond excessive political correctness. They often have needlessly large amounts of body piercings, gaudy hair colors, classify themselves as some obscure sexual or gender identity, and openly discuss mental health issues. Being different is fine, but doing anything and everything specifically to inflict oneself onto others is not simply "being different."

But to "be different" is to be "good" – and how will anyone know if no one can see it? Their desire to prove their goodness is compounded by a self-indulgent quest to advocate for their "unique" identity and experiences like religious mission work. They believe no one has suffered as they have, and they constantly seek to win in what some jokingly call "the oppression Olympics."

They see themselves as victims on a personal journey of discovering and rediscovering their victimhood. They believe being a victim is great because victims are "good." Moreover, the "victim" label functions as a moral justification for their expressions of rage, regardless of who is on the receiving end.

However, their explosive rage is actually a way to cope with (and mask) a misanthropic hopelessness that's hiding just below the surface. When they're not exploring their perceived victimhood or lashing out at those they see as privileged, they view the world and their fellow human beings with contempt.

They believe there's no future, that the planet is boiling over, resources are running out, and it's human beings fault! In their eyes, we are a cancer on the planet. They see the future as bleak.

They believe they can prove their goodness by using low-flush toilets or riding bicycles instead of driving cars. To punish society, to try to tell everyone else what they're doing wrong, they may vandalize prominent works of art or scream into social media, but it doesn't do much good.

All of this makes perfect sense if one believes that the future is dark and hopeless. This leads to a cycle: rage when you have the energy, and stew in self-doubt when you are too tired to rage anymore.

And, of course, there's always a great pastime to distract from self-hatred: drugs. Whether it's magic mushrooms, ecstasy, cocaine, opioids, marijuana, or just old-fashioned alcohol, if they just say they're going on a spiritual adventure to learn about themselves, it's definitely not a habit or a problem.

If they end up harming themselves or committing suicide, it's seen as evidence of their oppression, garnering more sympathy from a world they believe doesn't understand their hardships.

Apparently, we're all going to die anyway! There's no future for our racist settler colonial civilization founded on preserving cis-gender, hetero-centric patriarchy, so why not numb the brain to enjoy the ride?

Perhaps the worst thing: nothing stokes their rage more than seeing people taking care of themselves and striving to succeed or innovate. Exercise and physical fitness trigger them. People starting their own businesses or getting excited about new projects must be shut down. How dare these people be optimistic? How dare they be happy? How dare they not share the hopelessness and resentment that define their world?

If someone is confident, fit, optimistic, happy, or working toward something good, they must be stopped. They must be labeled as "fascist" or somehow a "bad" person. Such people, finding fulfillment in their lives, working to achieve goals, and having meaningful relationships with others cannot be allowed. Everything must be done to stop them at all costs.

Yes, they are willing to suddenly collaborate with people they deem toxic, including the US government, the police, and the military, if it means shutting down some confident, happy person out there. If they can "take down" someone who exudes a different vibe, that is one of the most important victories they can achieve. They might feel good for a day or even a week, but it's inevitably back to the same old hopeless cycle.

It's Not Just About Politics

We have all seen this type of person. It's not just about politics; it's a much deeper problem. It's a mindset that is being actively pumped out and cultivated at the highest levels. As people who want the best for ourselves, our families, our country, and our community, we are repelled by it.

But if we are honest with ourselves, we have our own share of it inside. We all do. What makes us different from the pink-haired menace is that while they embrace it, we are fighting against it. It might be harder on some days than others, but we are actively trying to suppress this pessimistic, destructive, rage-filled, depression-prone sentiment.

When we see the "woke" people, they horrify us. However, when they aren't attacking us and making our lives unpleasant, we have to admit we feel kind of sorry for them. They are useful in a way, as a negative example. This is what we would become if we ever gave up the fight. If we surrendered to the part of our minds that the social media apparatus and the richest and most powerful people are trying to pump up, we would be just like them—miserable—determined to make others miserable—repugnant, unpleasant, and hopeless.

We don't want to be that, and we know that. As hard as it might be, we have made a commitment to ourselves to not be this way. But we have realized that probably the most useful thing in not collapsing into this state of being is other people.

We can't do it alone. We need friends. We need our family. We need our community. We need our beliefs.

As much as we might get annoyed with the people around us, as much as we might disagree with them, or be disappointed by them, we need them. We don't just need other people; we need something to believe in.

Eurasia is Rising

Everything cannot be a lie. Everyone cannot be a fraud. Truth has to exist, and we need truth with which we can stand with other people… and with those other people, we need to BUILD.

We need to create. We need to perform. We need to beautify the world. We need to improve things. We need to help people. We need to feel a sense of satisfaction that comes from making a contribution.

It's not about making money. It's not about getting a better reputation; it's about taking the world around us and exerting our effort to improve it. We want living standards for the people in our community to go up. We want the level of material comfort and technological advancement to increase. We want people to live longer and have more children. We want life to be easier and more comfortable.

We want hope, we want community, we want truth, and we want growth.

The mindset that you are struggling day in and day out to cultivate within yourself—optimism, creativity, and the willingness to work with other people to achieve—is very much alive on the other side of the planet.

Russian President Vladimir Putin convened the World Youth Festival in Sochi in March of 2024 focused on tech innovation, economic expansion and the new BRICS economy around the world.

When I attended the *World Youth Festival* in 2024 in Sochi, Russia, I met with members of the All-China Youth Federation, the Ho Chi Minh Communist Youth Union of Vietnam, student organizations from across the African Continent, Russia's patriotic Movement of the First organization, the Robert Serra Youth Movement of Venezuela, among others. What I heard was a totally different tone. I heard love for their countries, hope for the future, and a belief in the power of humanity to better its conditions and strive for a higher plane.

Xi Jinping, China's President, recently proclaimed: "Whether in the past, present, or future, Chinese youth have always been and will always be at the forefront of propelling the great rejuvenation of the Chinese nation." Xi has referred to youth as the "spearhead and vital forces" in a wide range of projects crucial to the future of China and the world. He recently told students: "You should maintain firm ideals and convictions, work hard in study and training, hone your skills, and dedicate yourselves to serving as the loyal guardians of the Party and the people."

Technology and Economic Crisis

You are not alone in noticing that while significant parts of the world are progressing, there are significant issues in the

In China, youth are being mobilized to be part of a project of national rebirth and expansion.

West. Many people attribute this to some sort of conspiracy or cabal. Indeed, conspiracies do exist, and rich and powerful individuals often conspire among themselves to further their own conflicting interests.

However, we assert that the challenges facing Western civilization are not rooted in the malicious intent of individuals. Instead, they are rooted in economics.

Growth is beneficial, and technological development and growth should progress hand in hand. As technology advances, society's wealth should increase. Human beings should be able to move towards a more prosperous society with increasing abundance as technology diminishes the necessity for human labor.

Yet, this is not the current reality.

Consider self-driving cars, for instance. If car transportation could be entirely automated, it would be a positive development in a rational society. It would eliminate the chore of "driving," allowing human labor to be utilized elsewhere.

But that's not the society we live in. Andrew Yang explained it this way: "All you need is self-driving cars to destabilize society." He predicts that in a few years, "we're going to have a million truck drivers out of work who are 94 percent male, with an average level of education of high school or one year of college… We have five to 10 years before truckers lose their jobs," he said, "and all hell breaks loose." Something that should bring more prosperity and abundance is threatening to bring massive economic disaster.

As it becomes easier than ever to produce products in the age of 3D printers and significant technological breakthroughs, an age-old problem is emerging more prominently than ever: Poverty amid plenty, or poverty created by abundance.

There's a famous allegorical dialogue between a Polish coal miner and his son that goes like this:

> Son: Why is it so cold?
>
> Father: Because I cannot afford to buy any coal to heat the stove.
>
> Son: Why can't you afford to buy any coal?
>
> Father: Because I lost my job at the coal mine. I was laid off. I am unemployed.
>
> Son: Why did you lose your job? Why were you laid off?
>
> Father: Because there is too much coal.

Why should people be hungry because too much food has been created? Why should people be homeless because too much housing has been produced? Furthermore, why is the Biden administration working with gigantic financial institutions like BlackRock and strategizing with the World Economic Forum to reduce global crop outputs amid a pending crisis of malnutrition in Africa? Why are tent city encampments springing up across our country en masse, with people becoming homeless, as millions of empty apartments and houses can be found everywhere? Furthermore, why is the rent and cost of housing increasing at the same time?

We have an economic system in which the worker is never able to purchase what he produces.

Let's say you own a tire factory. A represents the materials necessary to create the tire, such as rubber, etc. B represents the costs of transporting the tires to where they are sold. C represents the human labor that is hired to assemble the tires. D represents the final cost of the tire when it is purchased.

$$A + B + C = D$$

Something is missing, of course. You, as the factory owner, need to make a profit. You cannot change how much the shipping costs. You cannot change how much the materials cost. You can only diminish the value put into the product by human labor. So, the equation should properly read this way:

$$A + B + C_1 + C_2 = D$$

Caleb Maupin, ideological leader of the Center for Political Innovation, explains the built in problems of production organized for profit.

C1 represents the wages paid out to the employees in the process of production. C2 represents the profit extracted from the labor value and taken as profit.

The worker is never paid the full value of the labor he puts into the product. This is the basis of Marxists' claim that the working class is exploited. Some might argue that the employer deserves compensation because he put up the money and created the enterprise. This is a separate point that diverts from the real problem inherent in this transaction. Beyond any perceived unfairness, the problem is this:

$$C1 < D$$

The worker is never paid enough in wages to purchase the product he produces. The wages paid out in the process of production are never enough to buy the products created.

This is called "overproduction" or "value crisis." The worker can never buy back what he produces. This is the basis of the boom and bust cycle.

However, the problem becomes intensified by technological advancement. In order to increase their profits, the owners of the industry are constantly looking to replace human labor with machines. Automation reduces labor costs. Corporations are competing with each other, trying to produce more efficiently and create more products.

But this leads to a bigger problem. Let's look at our equation:

$$A + B + C = D$$

$$A + B + C1 + C2 = D$$

If C, the human labor put into production, goes down, C2 decreases as well. The less human labor that is involved in the process of production, the less profit an employer can make.

This is called the "Tendency of the Rate of Profit to Fall" or "The Tendency of the Falling Rate of Profit." It forces the corporation to turn out even more products to make up for the decreased rate of profit per item sold.

These inherent problems in production organized for profit lead to a general rule of economic history, which is that when there is a huge leap in technology, the result is a long-term economic crisis. Jack Ma, the founder of Alibaba, observed this: "Technology is scary. The first technology revolution caused World War I. The second technology revolution caused, directly or indirectly, World War II. Now we are in the third technology revolution. What if a Third World War? If human beings do not have the same enemy, we will fight among ourselves. The enemy should be poverty… the enemy should be disease. I think that all those countries: China, Russia, USA, European, should share the technology, unite together to fight this war, and this is the war that, if we fight it together, young people will be much happier."

Jack Ma also remarked that technological leaps in Data Technology and Artificial intelligence can lead to a bright future and expansion of the spiritual and emotional existence, which really make us human: "Over the past one hundred years, we made people like machines. Now we make machines like people. But the right way to do it is to make over the next ten to twenty years a machine like a machine and people like people. A machine will never be able to conquer human beings. Machines are smart, machines are stronger and faster, but a machine does not have a soul, does not have values, does not have a belief that people have. So we should not make a machine think like a human being. We should make a machine learn like human beings."

Imperialism: A Global System of De-Growth

We do not live in the era of individual factory owners selling their products; we live in the age of gigantic corporations tied in with banks, stretching their tentacles all across the planet.

This global system of "trusts, cartels, and syndicates" dominating the economy, not just in their home countries but the planet itself, is called "imperialism." Imperialism is defined by the dominance of financiers. The age of "captains of industry" like Henry Ford or Andrew Carnegie is long gone. We now live in the era of bankers, and the primary way that the small clique of bankers that dominates the western world today stays in power is by holding back economic development.

While it would be normal for those who own businesses to want economic growth, the ultra-wealthy monopolists maintain their power by enacting degrowth. They want to impoverish the world and keep it poor so that they can stay on top.

The people of Mexico have been growing their food since before Christopher Columbus arrived in 1492. However, "Free Trade" policies of the North American Free Trade Agreement (NAFTA) put an end to that. The Mexican farming sector has been eliminated. Mexico has been "de-grown,"

Despite having a huge amount of natural petroleum wealth, the people of Africa's Niger Delta Region live in extreme poverty.

and Mexicans import their food from American agribusiness corporations.

More than a century ago, the British empire burned the vast textile looms of India and forced the people who had been weaving for centuries to import their cloth from Britain.

No African country exports more oil at this time than Nigeria. The Niger Delta Region is full of petroleum, one of the most vital commodities in our global economy. But the people of Nigeria live in utter poverty. The *CIA World Fact Book* describes a life expectancy of only 60 for males and 64 for females, with 53.7 infant deaths per live births. Only 62% of the adult population is literate. How can a country with so much natural wealth remain so impoverished?

The reality behind the global crisis is this: it is easier than ever before to churn out products. Human technology has created a more efficient process of production than ever before. The result is that millions of people have no place at the assembly line, the rate of profit for each product created has drastically decreased, and the billionaire financiers who run the world are in a desperate drive to "de-grow" the world, reduce living standards, reduce the population, and demolish their international competitors in order to stay at the top.

The countries targeted in US wars are all countries that have broken out of this disastrous economic setup and refused to be captive markets. Until 2011, it was not Nigeria, but Libya, that produced the most oil of any African country. Libya seized control of its oil resources in a popular revolution in 1969 led by Col. Moammar Gaddaffi. Libya had the highest life expectancy on the African continent and built the world's

In 2011, NATO bombing reduced Libya, which had the highest living standard on the African continent, to rubble and chaos.

largest irrigation system, "The Great Man-Made River," greening the desert with the goal of creating their own food. Africans from across the continent were trying to get to Libya to gain employment.

However, in 2011, Libya was destroyed by a US-backed "revolution." The country was forcibly "de-grown" with NATO bombs. Now the country is in ruin, with open-air slave markets, rival factions seizing territory, a lack of electricity, and economic devastation.

After the fall of the Soviet Union, the country was economically demolished. Farms went bankrupt. Factories shut their doors. Naomi Klein's study, *The Shock Doctrine*, explained that by 1998 "more than 80 percent of Russian farms had gone bankrupt, and roughly seventy thousand state factories had closed, creating an epidemic of unemployment." The number of Russians living below the poverty line reached 74 million during the late 90s, with Klein writing that "25 percent of Russians – almost 37 million people – lived in poverty described as 'desperate.'" The rate of drug addiction increased by 900%, and the suicide rate doubled.

As Russia was economically collapsing, the United States embraced it. Yeltsin and Clinton were noted for their close relationship, and US media and documentaries bragged about all the US "meddling" that made sure Yeltsin was re-elected in 1996.

The hatred for Russia in US media began when Putin came into office and started restructuring their economy. Putin put Gazprom and Rosneft, two state-controlled energy giants, at the center of the economy. The inflow of oil and gas revenue into the state budget enabled Russia to rebuild its industrial sector. During the first 8 years that Putin was in power, industrial output increased by 125%, and the country had finally reached the levels of production and growth it had during the time of the Soviet Union. The Russian GDP increased from $764 billion to $2096.8 billion between 2014 and 2017. The former CEO of British Petroleum, John Browne, observed: "No country has come so far, in such a short space of time."

With Russia once again a competitor, suddenly it became the object of scorn, demonization, and efforts to destabilize it from within yet again.

China was the "sick man of Asia" before 1949. At the time the Communists took power, China had very little electricity and not a single steel mill. Today, however, China makes half the world's steel. China has the world's largest telecommunications manufacturer, the world's fastest trains,

and the world's largest hydro-electrical power plant. Xi Jinping explained: "It is an essential requirement of socialism to eradicate poverty, improve people's living standards, and achieve common prosperity among the people."

China is making huge breakthroughs on the road to fusion energy; it produces the majority of the world's electric cars, and it has a vibrant and pioneering space program. After China's recent lunar launch, a French researcher named Pierre Yves-Meslin remarked: "It is a bit of a mystery to us how China has been able to develop such an ambitious and successful program in such a short time."

China was once a captive market, subdued by the British with two "Opium Wars" that prevented it from developing and building up its own economy. The China of the 1920s and 30s was one of mass starvation, illiteracy, sexual slavery, competing warlords, and drug gangs. But when China broke free, that started the process that led to creating what is now the second-largest economy in the world with over 800 million people lifted from poverty.

The imperialists want the world to be their impoverished captive market, but it is rapidly slipping out of their hands. The new economy emerging around the world with the BRICS is a threat to the monopoly of Wall Street and London, so they target it with sanctions, war, threat, and other schemes.

The results of the US-backed "regime change wars" or "revolutions" speak for themselves. As bad as Saddam Hussein may have been, no one can argue that Iraq today is better off. The NATO bombing and de-stabilization of Libya has reduced the country to ruin. The civil war the US fomenting in Syria hoping to topple the government resulted in millions of refugees and the rise of the terrorist group known as ISIS. US occupation of Afghanistan was 20 years of chaos with drug gangs and terrorist organizations getting stronger. From the fall of the Soviet Union, to Hillary Clinton's 2009 coup in Honduras, never has the destabilization of a country in the name of "human rights" brought a better life or improvement for the country subjected to "liberation." But the goal is always achieved, beating down an independent country and helping secure the global monopoly of the big western bankers and their governments.

Imperialism is all about degrowth. But they are bringing the degrowth home. What they once did to Africa, Asia, and Latin America, they are now doing to Pennsylvania, Ohio, Wisconsin, and Alabama. The roads are crumbling. The water isn't properly purified. The power plants are in shambles. Obama, Trump, and Biden all promised to revamp the country's infrastructure but failed to deliver. The heartland of the country is being hollowed out.

Why?

This is because the industrial middle class that once made America so prosperous is no longer needed. In the global, high-tech economy, there is no need for a layer of well-paid autoworkers, steelworkers, and manufacturers in the imperialist homeland. The USA is rapidly collapsing into a low-wage police state. The inflow of migrants, the rise of government surveillance, the sinister schemes dreamed up by the World Economic Forum about how you will "live in a pod," eat bugs, and "own nothing and be happy about it" are intended to save a dying system.

Degrowth is not socialism; it is highly controlled capitalism in which the productive forces are destroyed, and living standards are driven down in the hopes of stabilizing the system.

Tucker Carlson interviewed Chairman Omali Yeshitela of the African Peoples Socialist Party about the brutal FBI raid on his home and how he has been indicted, facing a possible15 years in prison.

One of the most blatant examples of the heavy-handed degrowth agenda of the US state has been the repression of the Uhuru movement. If one visits St. Petersburg, Florida, or St. Louis, Missouri, you will see a kind of Black community organizing that is very different from CNN's beloved George Soros "Black Lives Matter" mobs. The African Peoples Socialist Party and the Peoples Democratic Uhuru Movement have built a farmers market, classes for pregnant mothers, basketball courts, and other services to facilitate economic growth in the Black community. They have condemned the government welfare programs that maintain a state of defeated impoverishment among Black people and instead have pushed for the construction of a strong economy in Black neighborhoods and communities.

The response of the US government to this effort to bring about growth in some of America's poorest regions has been FBI repression. The FBI stormed into the homes of Omali Yeshitela and other organizers across the country. Drones were flown in, swats teams kicked down doors. Chairman

Omali described its this way: "In St. Louis, my wife and I were at our dining room table, preparing for her to attend a training session at the Uhuru House headquarters… Suddenly, a booming voice from the darkness startled us, instructing everyone to come out with their hands up and empty. The voice identified itself as the FBI, followed by explosions echoing throughout the neighborhood. As the explosions rattled the house, knocking plaster off the walls, it was initially difficult to believe the situation unfolding. I asked my wife to stay upstairs while I went to investigate and inform others, but communication was jammed, leaving us isolated. Upon descending, I was confronted with an armored personnel carrier and armed agents, reminiscent of a scene that ended tragically for Fred Hampton in Chicago years before. I felt the laser beams targeting me, convinced they were about to kill me. Fortunately, I made it downstairs without incident. However, my wife faced a drone as she opened the door, and both of us were quickly handcuffed. Confusion reigned as we demanded answers, only to be told of an impending indictment involving a Russian national, with our names somehow involved. They conducted a thorough search, seizing electronics and employing forceful tactics like battering rams and flashbang grenades. Similar raids were simultaneously carried out elsewhere, disrupting communities and instilling fear."

Now, three Americans, Omali Yeshitela, Penny Hess, and Jesse Nevel, face a possible sentence of 15 years in prison, charged as "Russian Agents." Their trial is set to begin on September 3rd. Tucker Carlson has spoken up about the case, as have many others. It is a blatant example of the government moving to crush economic development and free speech by accusing community organizers and advocates of economic empowerment of being "foreign agents" due to their statements about Ukraine.

The way Julian Assange has been brutally tortured just for giving a platform to those who would leak the dark secrets of the deep state reveals how little western leaders truly believe their rhetoric about "democracy" and "freedom."

The way January 6th protesters have been sentenced to astronomical amounts of time in prison for an event that was clearly arranged by more powerful forces, or the way students opposing Israeli crimes are facing expulsion and police brutality, all reveal what the agenda of the big monopolies and their government truly is.

They have a vision for a high-tech dark ages, abolishing our freedom to preserve their profits, as they march humanity toward a new world war. We must resist this scheme with all of our might, as we come to understand the roots of the crisis.

The Road to Freedom is Abundance

The "woke" ideology, being utilized to rally young people to push for destruction, is not standard or classical Marxism. It has very little in common with what was carried out by Stalin, Mao, Castro, or other Marxist-Leninist political leaders in the 20th century.

Stalin mobilized the Soviet people to rapidly build and industrialize. The communist governments of the 20th century were all focused on increasing productive forces, raising living standards, building universities, and modernizing their countries. Whatever shortcomings they had, it cannot be denied that aside from a few outliers like Pol Pot, Communism has been a pro-growth movement.

In fact, the vision of "the higher stage of communism" laid out by Marx is very much a post-scarcity society in which growth has zoomed to higher levels than ever before. Marx wrote in *Critique of the Gotha Program*: "Right can never be higher than the economic structure of society and its cultural development conditioned thereby. In a higher phase of communist society, after the enslaving subordination of the individual to the division of labor, and therewith also the antithesis between mental and physical labor, has vanished; after labor has become not only a means of life but life's prime want; after the productive forces have also increased with the all-around development of the individual, and all the springs of co-operative wealth flow more abundantly – only then can the narrow horizon of bourgeois right be crossed in its entirety and society inscribe on its banners: From each according to his ability, to each according to his needs!"

A society in which "labor becomes life's prime want," meaning that technology has increased to the point that people only work because they want to, a society where the "springs of cooperative wealth flow more abundantly," this is the ultimate pro-growth vision. The breakdown of inequality, as Marx envisioned it, was not intended to be forced, but rather to come about as an all-around expansion of human productivity.

This is what was behind Deng Xiaoping's famous statement "Poverty is not socialism, but to be rich is glorious." You cannot create equality with willpower or force. The basis of oppression, enforced social hierarchies, and state power is scarcity. The road to freedom is abundance and economic expansion.

History has shown us this. Human rights did not appear out of nowhere. The reason talk of "the rights of man" did not arise until Europe in the 1500s is not because humans were just evil until that point. It was with a new level of economic development that a new level of freedom could be realized. The rise of capitalism was a great advance over feudalism, just as feudalism was a great advance over slavery.

Human beings are constantly marching toward a higher plane of development, more efficiently forcing the environment to serve us, expanding our population and living standards. As we advance our technology, we constantly reinvent our social systems. As society becomes more abundant, the population increases, as we live longer, we become more free.

Separating "human rights" from economic development is one of the biggest deceptions of the western liberal order. It frames "freedom" as a question of abstract morality, completely disregarding the conditions in which state structures are created and social contracts are forged. Western leaders impose crippling sanctions on countries, justifying it with rhetoric about how the peoples of the targeted countries are having their human rights violated. Does it not occur to US leaders that a lack of development, a lack of foreign trade, is itself a big factor in human rights being restricted? How do western leaders expect a society to become more "free" if its ability to decrease poverty and develop is cut off?

During the 1950s, the CIA began reinventing leftist politics with its Congress for Cultural Freedom program. The Frankfurt School and academic post-modernism trace their roots back to this effort to subvert genuine socialist movements.

Where did "Woke" come from?

Woke-ism is the result of a sinister project of manipulating politics that started with intelligence agencies. The CIA's *Congress for Cultural Freedom* Program began in the 1950s. The US government began coordinating with Rockefeller think tanks and the Ford Foundation to reinvent the political "left" and separate it from economic questions. The CIA funded magazines like *Encounter* and *Partisan Review* and brought us the Frankfurt School, a new brand commonly called "Cultural Marxism."

The focus of this new brand was not on mobilizing the working class to seize control of the means of production and raise productive forces, but instead, demonizing the bulk of the population as a tyrannical ignorant mob and celebrating non-conformity. Adorno's *Authoritarian Personality*, Marcuse's *One Dimensional Man*, and Arendt's *Eichmann in Jerusalem* have nothing to do with the popular movements that built labor unions or fought against colonialism. These are elitist screeds of a middle class that sees the bulk of the population with contempt and fear and seeks to control them. The striving of the people to see their living standards increase and to not have big bankers rip them off and loot their country is deemed "fascism."

Woke-ism, with its shrill contempt for the bulk of the population and its pessimistic view of the future, takes elements of Trotskyism, the French Revolution's guillotine bloodlust, the natural rebelliousness of teenagers, and synthesizes it into a deadly cocktail for breaking people psychologically and helping set the stage for the low-wage, degrowth police state Wall Street and London are looking to set up.

The sinister role of Zionism cannot be ignored either. While Marxists called for the Jewish people to merge and assimilate with the rest of the working class and strive for a socialist society free of bigotry and discrimination of any kind, Zionism maintained that Jews were a special elite group that could never fit in with European civilization and needed their own state. Zionism is the original anti-populism. It was Lenin who once described it as "the spirit of the ghetto," the call for Jews to exist as a separate group with a separate state. The way Israel is given billions of American taxpayer dollars each year, loads of free weapons, and protection from the United States as it shocks the world with criminal actions in Gaza fits in with the overall dark, degrowth vision of the dying imperialist system.

Woke-ism and the corresponding economic philosophy of degrowth is a reinvention of fascist economics. As the Nazis rebooted Germany's economy temporarily with military spending and the creation of a slave labor underclass, the woke element and the Silicon Valley elites that put their message on blast want to save their system from a crisis of overproduction by attempting to grind the wheels of history backward. It is a hopeless endeavor that can only be temporarily successful, coming at a massive cost in terms of basic humanity.

Many American working people dislike woke-ism and its pessimistic and dark message. It appears that as anti-woke blowback brews among the working class, the ruling elite are trying to manipulate these sentiments as well. Even though many people voted for Trump because he said he would stop American involvement in foreign wars, Trump supporters are being manipulated and channeled into supporting the heavy handed repression of college protesters who want an end to US support for Israel. The idea that woke-ism is somehow a big conspiracy from China, not from the ultra-rich on Wall

*The Port of Qinzhou has been built using the growth mindset of the
Government of China*

Street and in Silicon Valley is also pushed very hard in
conservative circles.

Anyone who has been to China, Russia, Vietnam, Cuba,
Iran, Venezuela or any of the anti-imperialist countries knows
that their ideology and way of living in resistance to the dying
global order of western bankers has nothing in common with
the pessimistic "woke" trend. This is being intentionally
distorted by pro-war and pro-Israel conservatives. A toxic
"anti-woke" brand that pushes "survival of the fittest" market
individualism and lies to justify regime change wars is likely
to grow more prominent in the coming years. This must be
opposed and exposed for the deception that it is.

A Government of Action

So, what can be done? We need a society where growth is promoted. We need a society where human creativity and brilliance are unleashed, not stifled and restrained. We need a society where the economy is rationally organized to ensure constant growth.

21st Century Socialism, the Socialist Oriented Market Economy of Vietnam, or Socialism with Chinese Characteristics are adjustments. They are not the old Soviet model. They have plenty of room for tech developers, entrepreneurs, and innovators. In fact, the state goes out of its way to subsidize and promote the middle-class layer of independent creators. The strength of socialism in Nicaragua has been its micro-entrepreneurship program, enabling thousands of people to start their own businesses, launch their own cooperatives, and be subsidized in doing so to make the country wealthier overall.

The difference between capitalism and socialism is not the role of government. State ownership and taxation exist in all societies to some degree or another. Socialism is not the redistribution of wealth. All governments "tax and spend" to some degree or another.

Some capitalist societies like Saudi Arabia and Singapore have a huge amount of state oversight and control of the economy. Others, like the United States, have a tradition of a more laissez-faire approach.

The question of capitalism or socialism is rooted in the purpose for which production is organized. Friedrich Engels stated that "under capitalism, the means of production only

China has been pushing the boundaries of fission and fusion by pursuing the growth Nuclear Power would unlock

function as preliminary transformation into capital." Marx spoke of the "anarchy of production." Mao Zedong described capitalism as a system of "profits in command."

Capitalism is an economy where the drive of owners to make profits dictates economic activity. Socialism is when society overall controls the means of production to ensure growth is not restricted. Socialism is when a government of action leads a well-organized population to organize the economy and control it so growth is constant and never restrained.

The creation of a "government of action" in the United States would fulfill the American revolution. The very basis of the war of independence was the desire of the people for an economy that was not simply a trading hub in the British sea-based empire of plunder. The American people wanted their own economy, they wanted westward expansion, they wanted GROWTH.

The Civil War continued this battle, as the Confederate Slavocracy, which banned looms and discouraged technological development, sought to maintain a primitive agrarian economy that could supply cheap cotton to the British textile monopolies. Abraham Lincoln led a coalition of small farmers, industrialists, labor unionists, abolitionists, and slave revolutionaries like Harriet Tubman and Frederick Douglas to smash the plantation system and its Wall Street allies. The US Civil War was the Second American Revolution, and the Republican Party newspaper of New York City, *The New York Tribune*, hired Karl Marx as its London correspondent. Marx wrote glowing articles about Lincoln as "the single-minded son of the working class," and Communist August Willich rose up to the rank of Brigadier General.

It should be noted that the US Civil War and the American revolution itself were both preceded by mass episodes of spiritual rebirth. The First and Second Great Awakenings were explosions of Christian revivalism that called for the country to turn around, repent from its ways, and recommit itself to the principles of equality and justice.

The Center for Political Innovation puts forward a 4-point economic plan to restore the US economy:

1. A mass program to rebuild our country:

Hire the unemployed and put them to work rebuilding the crumbling roads, bridges, schools, and hospitals of the country. Construct high-speed railways, new universities, new power plants, and give the country an overall tech upgrade to let innovation flourish.

2. Public control of our natural resources:

The oil, gas, coal, and timber of America, the natural wealth flowing from the country's soil, should be utilized to make the country overall wealthier, not to enrich Wall Street firms. Utilizing our natural resources to fund the public budget would take the burden of taxation off the population.

3. Public control of banking & canceling of debt:

A national bank as well as state and local banks should have a monopoly on credit and lend money strategically as part of an overall plan to expand the living standards and production. The debt that hangs over the economy as a curse must be lifted. The printing of money must be handled by the public, not the Federal Reserve rip-off system.

4. An economic bill of rights:

Similar to that proposed by Roosevelt in his final State of the Union address. To ensure a strong economy in the United States, the labor power of every person must be utilized, healthcare must be made available to all, quality education must be provided. This shouldn't be seen as a handout or charity but rather as an investment in the nation. It is human labor and human creativity that are the sources of all wealth and expansion, and human beings must be properly cultivated to make a more prosperous country.

We believe in growth. A new economy is rising around the world, and in China, Russia, Vietnam, Cuba, Nicaragua, Venezuela, Iran, Syria, and the other countries that continue to resist the all-out war drive against them from Wall Street, growth is also the priority.

Too many people exist in a dark, pessimistic state of being, left behind by a society that has no place for them. In our high-tech world, the strengths of every individual can be utilized to make life more beautiful. The narrow limits and artificial restrictions imposed by the dominion of ultra-monopolists must be broken.

China is not our enemy. Our enemy is an outdated, irrational system where the chaos of the market takes precedence over humanity's intrinsic need and drive to expand to greater heights.

A new world, beyond imperialism, where countries trade with each other on the basis of win-win cooperation, and all humanity marches toward a world without scarcity or state coercion can be realized.

The Center for Political Innovation recently led the US delegation to the World Youth Festival in Sochi, Russia. At the gathering, Russian President Putin said the following: "So, we are all born equal, but the question is, do we grow and develop under equal conditions? The answer is, unfortunately, not. This is the greatest injustice in today's world order. If you ask me what can be done for everybody to live and grow under equal conditions, unlocking their talents for the benefit of their loved ones, their family, their country, and perhaps humanity as a whole, I do not know. But what I do know for certain is that we all must strive for it. Only by striving for it will we make the world more transparent, just, democratic, sustainable, balanced, and safe."

Let us oppose war. Let us oppose state repression and the attacks on our civil liberties. Let us demand a government of action that fights for working families. Let us work to build greater abundance and greater freedom than has ever been imagined.

- The Members of the Center for Political Innovation

CPI Press Conference at the UN

February 15th, 2024 the Russian Mission to the United Nations sponsored a press conference where the American participants in the World Youth Festival presented and expressed their concerns about US government criminalization of solidarity with Russia. These were Caleb Maupin's opening remarks to the official UN press conference.

In October, I was deeply honored when the youth office of the Russian foreign ministry reached out to me about forming a national preparatory committee for the upcoming World Youth Festival set for March in Russia. As someone who attended the World Festival of Youth and Students in 2013 in Quito, Ecuador, and the festival held in Sochi in 2017, as an advocate of socialism, peace, and international cooperation, as an American patriot, as a Christian, and as someone who strives to live according to the teachings of Jesus Christ, I considered this to be a great opportunity.

However, it is the circumstances of our upcoming trip that bring us here today. As we meet here today, Jesse Neville, Penny Hess, and Omali Yeshitela have been indicted by the U.S. Department of Justice. They are facing a possible 15 years in prison. Their trial date was just set for September. The Biden administration has charged them for doing what we are about to do: for going to an international conference in Russia. The Biden administration has declared that putting on some Zoom calls and writing some articles about Ukraine has been a conspiracy to act as a foreign agent.

This case is absolutely outrageous. It's an attack on freedom of assembly, freedom to travel, freedom of speech, and freedom of association, and it's designed to intimidate Americans from doing what we plan to do: visit Russia and question U.S. foreign policy. In light of this horrific indictment, it is very important that we go to Russia to show that we will not be intimidated and to take responsibility for the future amid the utter failure of the Biden administration.

Biden said he would end the war in Yemen, and as we all know now, that war is expanding, and U.S. bombs are being dropped on Yemen. Biden has poured billions of dollars of American taxpayer money into Ukraine to prolong this war, at the same time that our bridges and highways are crumbling, our living standards are dropping, and American working families are being squeezed by inflation. Under these circumstances, with Biden trying to intimidate Americans and weaponizing the Department of Justice against dissidents and with international tensions rising, we have a duty to go to Russia and show the world another America.

Because there are two Americas. Beyond Wall Street and Hollywood, in the vast territories of the American heartland, you will find a lot of hardworking people who love their children, love their communities, and want a better life. You will find an America that values peace, not war. It is this America that produced Dr. Martin Luther King Jr., the Black Panthers, the great abolitionist John Brown, and it is this America that produced the labor movement that pushed forward Roosevelt, the great anti-fascist coalition that propelled the United States to align with the Soviet Union to defeat the menace of fascism, and a great moment in history also to align with China.

It is this America, the America that's been hidden from mainstream TV, the America that has been canceled by these social media monopolies. It's this America of the working class, of small business owners, and people of many different races and ethnic backgrounds who reject war and the emerging low-wage police state. It is this America and its democratic traditions that I will be proudly representing in Sochi.

There's a new economy arising in the world today, centered around the BRICS, the Eurasian Economic Union, the Belt and Road Initiative of China, and the real America would benefit from joining with this new economy, trading with countries on the basis of win-win cooperation, and ending the wars, the threats, and the sanctions.

The Center for Political Innovation sees Russia as an ally of the real America, and we call for the charges against the

Uhuru 3 to be immediately dropped. We look forward to making lots of new friends at the upcoming World Youth Festival, not just youth from Russia but youth from the 188 different countries that will be represented at this vitally important international gathering.

Thank you.

"No One Knows Where!": Marxism and Creativity

The following is a transcript of Caleb Maupin's address to the First National Convention of the Center for Political Innovation in Portland, Oregon on December 2nd, 2023.

Wow, what an amazing conference this is! Our first national Convention of the Center for Political Innovation, and I'm overjoyed. I would like Elizabeth to stand up. Yes, because there's a very important issue that we've been discussing with the board of directors. And that is, we have determined after intense debate and negotiation that one does not have to have red hair in order to be in the leadership of the Center for Political Innovation. We will allow non-gingers into leadership. It is allowed. You know, you're going to be careful though, but it'll be allowed.

But in all seriousness, you guys have no idea how much work Elizabeth has done. You really have no idea. I just found out today that she personally made every single one of those banners. Each one of those represents 10 hours of work from Elizabeth. Elizabeth found this venue, she did so much. We are in deep appreciation for all that she has done, not just for this convention but for this organization. We are proud to call her our president. This is the leader of the Center for Political Innovation right here, Elizabeth Young, Thank you, Thank you!

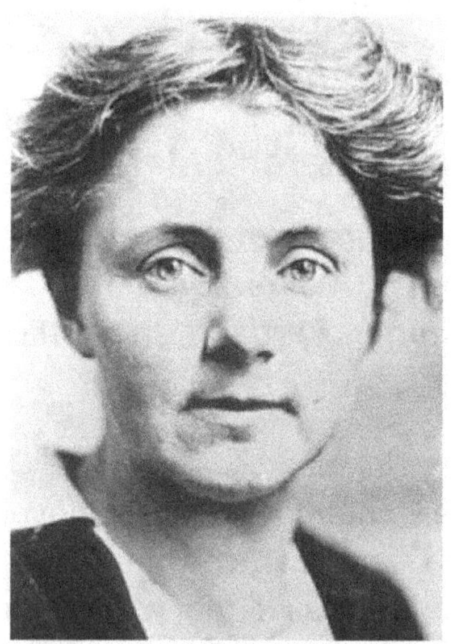

American writer Anna Louise Strong, who eventually moved to Russia and China wrote about how socialism and anti-imperialism align with the American spirit.

Anna Louise Strong

Now, everyone who's wearing a red scarf, could you please stand up? Yes, these are the members of the CPI who helped put on and convene the conference. And we decided to get red scarves and we also have buttons. Does someone have one of the buttons? The button here, it says Anna Louise Strong Brigade. That's what we decided to call the members of the CPI that came to town to convene the conference. That's Anna Louise Strong. And this is an American that so many people don't know anything about. She's a name that's kind of been written out of the history books.

But she's been pivotal, not just in the history of this country but in the history of the world. Anna Louise Strong was from this part of the country and was a key leader of the Seattle General Strike in 1919. She was the main journalist for the *Union Record*, which was the wobbly labor paper in Seattle. And then after the strike was defeated, she heard about this new country that was created called the Soviet Union and she went over there and saw the amazing things that they were achieving. She came back to the United States and wrote books about it, went on speaking tours about it. And eventually, she moved to Moscow and she was the editor of *The Moscow News*, which was the English language newspaper that they had in Moscow in the 1930s.

So, I like to say she was RT before RT. She's "old school" RT right here. And Anna Louise Strong eventually moved to China and she interviewed Mao Zedong. And it was in her interview with Mao that he first used the phrase "paper tigers" to describe the imperialists.

She was not loved in this country due to McCarthyism, so she spent her final years in China. And in China, she was known as the paper tiger lady. Mao Zedong and Zhou Enlai and other key leaders of the Chinese Communist Party would come over to her house all the time to consult with her on politics. She really comprehended economics and political theory. She was also deeply poetic. Her writing is deeply beautiful.

And it was discovering her writing as a teenager that I discovered her autobiography, *I Change Worlds*, her memoir of living in the Soviet Union called *The Stalin Era*, her writing, *The Soviets Expected It*, about World War II. She wrote so much about the socialist movement and what it's about. And in everything she wrote, she brought with it a spirit of Americanism. She was not ashamed to be an American. She knew this country did a lot of evil things, but there was Americanism that just flowed through everything that she wrote.

I'm going to read to you something that this amazing woman, who's been left out of US history, wrote. And this was at the time that that great Seattle General Strike was happening. This is what she wrote, this is an editorial she wrote for *The Seattle Union Record*. She said:

We do not need hysteria.

We need the iron march of labor.

LABOR WILL FEED THE PEOPLE.

Twelve great kitchens have been offered, and from them food will be distributed by the provision trades at low cost to all.

LABOR WILL CARE FOR THE BABIES AND THE SICK.

NOT THE WITHDRAWAL OF LABOR POWER, BUT THE POWER OF THE WORKERS TO MANAGE WILL WIN THIS STRIKE.

The closing down of Seattle's industries, as a **MERE SHUTDOWN,** will not affect these eastern gentlemen much. They could let the whole northwest go to pieces, as far as money alone is concerned.

BUT, the closing down of the capitalistically controlled industries of Seattle, while the **WORKERS ORGANIZE** to feed the people, to care for the babies and the sick, to preserve order— **THIS** will move them, for this looks too much like the taking over of **POWER** by the workers.

Labor will not only **SHUT DOWN** the industries, but Labor will **REOPEN;** under the management of the appropriate trades, such activities as are needed to preserve public heath and public peace. If the strike continues, Labor may feel led to avoid public suffering by reopening more and more activities,

UNDER ITS OWN MANAGEMENT.

And that is why we say that we are starting on a road that leads—NO ONE KNOWS WHERE!

That's Anna Louise Strong in 1919 talking about how the potential of the strike wasn't going to be from creating disorder, wasn't going to be from creating chaos. It would be about the new beautiful order that emerged when working people stepped up and started taking responsibility and taking participation in the leadership of their society. That the strike would preserve and present a new order. That's what she was writing about. She was a city builder, Anna Louise Strong.

An Age of Pessimism

And we live in an age where there's so much pessimism. And a lot has been said about this.

I won't be the first person to make this comparison, but the time period we're living in is a lot like the lead-up to the First World War. War brings out the worst in people and it makes people hopeless about humanity. It makes people question what it's all worth.

There's a poem that they used to make boomers memorize in school. They don't do that anymore. That's a thing they used to do, is they used to make kids memorize poems in school. And there's one poem that used to make kids memorize, and because it was so widely taught in school, people make fun of it a lot. So, you've probably heard people reference it. And it goes like this:

I think that I shall never see
A poem lovely as a tree.

A tree whose hungry mouth is prest
Against the earth's sweet flowing breast;

A tree that looks at God all day,
And lifts her leafy arms to pray;

A tree that may in Summer wear
A nest of robins in her hair;

Upon whose bosom snow has lain;
Who intimately lives with rain.

Poems are made by fools like me,
But only God can make a tree.

Well, that was written by Joyce Kilmer and he was shot in the head during World War I. That poem expressed the pessimism of the age. It expressed the belief that all this technological advancement, all this progress, wasn't really leading to a beautiful new world. Instead, it was just giving us new weapons with which to kill each other, new technology with which to gun each other down. It was looking to Nature, looking with defeat at Humanity. "Only God Can Make A Tree", looking at human progress, looking at the idea that we can advance as a species with pessimism and cynicism and hopelessness. It's a cry of defeat.

And as I said, war brings out the worst in people. You know, my grandfather, he fought in the Second World War and he went into the US Marine Corps. He was from a small town in Missouri and he and all the other young men from his small town in rural Missouri, they went into the US Marine Corps. My grandfather hated the US Marine Corps. He would see a billboard for the Marines or he would hear the Marine hymn and he would get angry, visibly angry. He hated the basic training that they went through. It was very brutal.

He went through basic training and they gave him an IQ intelligence test and he tested pretty high so they switched him into the US Navy. He was an officer in the US Navy. So then after the war he went to try and meet up with all the young men who had fought with him in the US Marines. But he couldn't meet with them because they were almost all dead. All of them had died except for one.

He met with the one surviving member of his unit in the US Marines and the guy was visibly not well. And in the conversation they had when they had dinner, he bragged to my grandfather about all the gold that he had pulled out of the teeth of Japanese corpses during the war. And my grandfather heard that and he was just hurt by that.

My grandfather was in the US Navy. He was a Navy officer during the war and he also told us the story of how one day he was getting his hair cut uh and he was getting his hair cut and a torpedo hit his ship. It blew off the front of the ship off. And then as he was right there getting his haircut he gasped as a torpedo came through the wall and didn't explode. It didn't go off.

Marxism is a Celebration of Human Creativity

In that moment he thought he was going to die. And a couple men had died when the torpedo hit the front of the ship and he survived. And my grandfather, the deep visual hatred he had for the US Marine Corps, that was a result of seeing the very same things that that motivated Joyce Kilmer, the very same things that Rosa Luxemberg wrote about and was describing when she wrote about "Socialism or barbarism."

She said that imperialism left unhinged up to its natural capacity would lead to "desolation, degeneration, depopulation, and a great cemetery" in Europe. It would lead to civilizations coming apart. So he was describing what Friedrich Nietzsche talks about when he talks about the "blonde beast" and how by becoming a colonizer and an imperialist the Western man was losing any pretense of being civilized, any moral code. It was becoming the law of the jungle once again. Might makes right; cruelty, the thriving of the most sadistic and vicious elements.

That's what imperialism was leading to and in imperialist Wars we see that ugliness come out and that's what drives a lot of the pessimism that we saw and the lead up to the First World War.

Marxism is the opposite. Marxism is a celebration of human creativity. Friedrich Engels, he said "the animal merely uses its environment and brings about changes in it simply by its presence, but man by his changes, makes it serve his ends, masters it, and this is the final distinction between man and other animals, and it is labor that brings about this distinction."

What's he saying there? He's saying that ants have been making their ant farms the same way for thousands of years. Beavers have been making their beaver dams the same way for thousands of years. But in just 5, 6, 7, 8 thousand years human beings have gone from hunter gatherers in the woods to space travel and iPhones. We are constantly reinventing our relationship with our environment. We are constantly expanding our population, expanding our living standard, providing a more comfortable life. What makes human beings unique is that we are constantly reinventing our relationship with nature, to build build a better life. No other species that we're aware of anywhere in the universe is capable of doing what human beings are doing are capable of doing. This is a Godlike creative power that other species do not have. That's something to celebrate and that's something to be optimistic about.

Marxism teaches us that hunter gatherer civilization was around for a long time but we got too good at hunter gatherer civilization. With our sticks and rocks we were killing animals pretty effectively, with our ability to track plants and how they grow; our ability to gather fruits and nuts; we got so good at it so there was a scarcity. So, we reinvented our relationship with nature and we started growing our own crops and domesticating animals. We reinvented our relationship to get to a higher mode. Feudalism was an outmoded system and so again we had another Social Revolution to get us to a higher mode of existence, so we could create and build better things.

Marxism has us understanding what the problem that we're in right now. We are living in a prolonged crisis of overproduction and the fall rate of profit. This should be a widespread understanding. Its pretty basic.

If you read old pamphlets from the 1930s, if you asked Anna Louise Strong or William Z. Foster or Huey Long or Fred Hampton they would tell you this in a heartbeat. They knew this stuff. They knew it like the back of their hand, yet no one talks this way anymore. No one except for the Center for Political Innovation.

We're the only ones that talk about this. The Communist Parties around the world that make up the World Anti-Imperialist platform they say in their documents that the crisis facing society is a crisis of overproduction, and that's what it is. The capitalist is constantly trying to produce as many goods as he possibly can and pay the worker as little as he possibly can in the process of doing it. Then the worker doesn't have enough to buy back what he produces.

In a rational society self-driving cars would be a great thing because this job called driving wouldn't be necessary and human labor would be much more productive. But in capitalism self-driving cars would lead to as Andrew Yang put it, to riots in the streets. Self-driving cars would be a society-wide crisis and the fact that we're just a couple years away from self-driving cars is hanging over our economy like a curse. This isn't rational.

In systems of the past, people were homeless because there wasn't enough housing. Only under capitalism are people homeless because there is too much housing. In systems of the past, people were hungry because there wasn't enough food but only under capitalism are people hungry because there is too much food.

The artificial intelligence computer revolution, the great dynamic breakthroughs in technology that we've created, they have outstripped the narrow limits and restraints of the capitalist system. Human creativity and human ability to reinvent our relationship with Mother Nature and to strive for a higher and more efficient mode of production, is no longer able to fit into the narrow restraints this economy. This is an economy where profit for private owners defines production. That is what is driving the crisis that is leading to dropping living standards.

This is what is causing the crisis of global migration. This is what is causing the capitalists of the United States to become more aggressive and push for a new world war around the world. This is what is causing the capitalist of the United States to fight with each other like they've never fought before and generations. It's all rooted in this problem of over production and the tendency of the falling rate of profit.

The Frustration of Youth

The answer isn't degrowth! The answer isn't to go backward! The answer isn't to say there's something inherently wrong with human progress! The answer is to say that we need to liberate the creativity of the next generation from the artificial restrictions and the narrow restraint to the profit system.

One thing that we see a lot of now is frustrated creative youth. Young people, young men, young women who know that they're capable of doing something great. There's probably a young person right now sweeping the floor at McDonald's or doing some other job where they're

Carl Geiser, born in Orrville, Ohio, became an important leader of the Abraham Lincoln Brigade, anti-fascist volunteers who fought in Spain.

miserable. They are saying to themselves "I'm miserable because I know I could be doing something beautiful right now! I could be designing something! I could be studying engineering! I could be studying science! I I have something to contribute, but all my society has given me is a low wage short-term service sector job. It's given me a phone to dazzle me. It's legalized all kinds of drugs that I can use and screw myself up with. My potential is not being utilized!" That is a frustration that so many young people have in this country right now.

They say young people are lazy, they don't want to do anything. Bullshit! People who are 19-years-old, 20-years-old, 22, 23, that's when they want to go out and do things! But because some boss can't make a profit hiring them to do it, they don't get to do it. They exist in this state of frustration. They say "I'm capable of something more! I have potential inside of me and my society isn't letting me get it out!" That feeling is all over this country. If you want to talk about all the problems that we've got with opioids and suicide and shooters, you look at that frustrated creativity. When people want to go build and create, they're told "no room for you" it is the worst feeling in the world.

Communists: The Ones Who Mean It

I'm a little older now I'm not officially a youth anymore. I'm going to be 36 in a few days. I'm not officially a youth anymore, but I know what it's like to be a frustrated creative young person. That's how I found out about this guy. [Holds up picture of Carl Geiser]

I was a frustrated creative teenager in know Ohio I was 13 or 14-years-old, and I was bored. So I got on the internet and I thought that I would look and see if in the little town in Ohio, if there had ever been another Communist in that town.

I grew up in a town called Orrville. It's where Smuckers Jelly comes from. Its the home of Bobby Knight the basketball coach, that's the celebrity that that we claim. So, I just thought I would search the internet to see if there had ever been another Communist from my little town of 10,000 people in Orrville, Ohio.

That's how I found out about Carl Geiser. He was born in Orrville Ohio. He went to Orrville High School and he was a pretty high achieving student. So he went to Cleveland State University and he studied electrical engineering. He graduated and he became an electrical engineer. But the United States was having at that point, the Great Depression. There weren't many jobs for electrical engineers. But there was another country where there were a lot of jobs for electrical engineers, that was the Soviet Union. He went over to the Soviet Union to help Stalin set up those new hydroelectric power plants that they were building, to electrify parts of the country that had never had electrification before.

Lenin said "Communism is Soviet Power Plus Electrification" and in the 1930s, Stalin was doing it. The world was astonished at the rapid industrialization, as the USSR became an industrial power house in a few short years.

Carl Geiser was blown away by what he saw and he came back to the United States from the Soviet Union and he joined the Communist Party. He joined the Communist party because he saw what socialism was achieving. A lot of people joined the Communist Party in these years for the same reason.

But Carl Geiser went a bit further, he joined the Abraham Lincoln Brigade. When fascists were looking to overthrow the Spanish Republic, the Communists of Spain called for their comrades around the world to come and volunteer to fight fascism in Spain. Thousands of young American men went to Spain and fought.

Carl Geiser was actually taken prisoner and he was a prisoner of war in fascist Spain. He almost died, if they had found out what his rank actually was they would have shot him, but his comrades concealed his rank. Eventually, Roosevelt got him traded back to the United States in a prisoner exchange. He came back to United States and he's a hero of Anti-Fascism and the Spanish Civil War, a leader of the Abraham Lincoln Brigade.

When you think about the Abraham Lincoln Brigade, that points to an aspect of our movement that it's really important to understand. There's a famous writer named Sherwood Anderson, a novelist, he wrote *Winesburg Ohio*. At one point Sherwood Anderson was asked "What's the difference between a socialist and a communist?" He said "I don't know the technical difference, but it seems to me like the Communists, they're the ones who mean it."

What he was pointing to was the fact that when we do something, we really do it. In the early 1930s, the understanding was that the Social Democrats and the reformists, the sellout leaders who had betrayed the revolution in Germany, they were leading workers to oppose the Soviet Union in the name of socialism; they were the main threat. The feeling was that it was necessary to expose the Social Democrats and the reformists and that was the line in the Communist International. We didn't just half ass oppose the Social Democrats, we didn't just sort-of oppose the Social Democrats. We went all in. We really opposed the Social Democrats, because we understood that that was what was necessary. All over the world Communists went into "class against class" mode to expose the Social Democrats and build a United Front From Below because we understood that that was the correct tactic.

After the rise of Hitler and as the situation changed, the line changed, and it became correct to align with the Social Democrats in the United Front against Fascism. When that line changed, we didn't just half-ass align with them against fascism. What did we do? We built the Abraham Lincoln Brigade. We went and fought in Spain. We had the Battle of Cable Street in London. We built huge anti-fascist mobilizations. We are the reason Roosevelt won the 1936 presidential election.

When we do something, we do it hard! There was a labor leader once remarked "If it's 3 in the morning at your labor union hall and there's two guys running the mimeograph machine, you can bet at least one of them is a communist!"

The people who criticize our movement, one of the most common critiques from Trotskyites and others is "They Zigzag! They're always reversing themselves!"

They are right. Yeah, if the situation changes in 24 hours the tactics must also change in 24 hours. Sometimes what's correct on Monday is not correct on Tuesday and it's not correct on Wednesday. When you are fully committed to achieving what we aim to achieve, it can look a little strange to people who don't get it. They can go, "Well, one day you're running this way, and the next day you're running this way." Yes, and every way that we run, we're running hard because we understand that it's necessary and that it must be done.

The Peace Puppets — Building A Community of Resistance

And that brings me to a story or a bit of wisdom that was passed down to me. You know, we can be critical of different figures, but Sam Marcy, an important leader of Communism in the post-war years, he would often talk about how at the anti-war protests that happened during the 1960s, where you'd have hundreds of thousands of people marching against the Vietnam War, there'd be these beautiful puppets that they would build. They'd have puppets of Richard Nixon with his money or whatever. They'd have puppets of the heroic Vietnamese people fighting for their liberation. These beautiful puppets were a big part of anti-war rallies.

Marcy often used the example of the activists who created puppets for rallies against the Vietnam War as an example of an anti-imperialist community.

There were whole communities of people, and they weren't members of any communist group, but they were against the Vietnam War and had a general leftist anti-imperialist view. And they made it their mission that when there was a big anti-war rally, they would come together and they would make these beautiful works of art as their contribution to opposing the war in Vietnam. And there were whole communities that built these puppets. It was their project, their way of being creative, of building community and coming together.

There were couples who met each other through the process of making those puppets, and a couple years later, they were there making the puppets with their little kids that they had just had. And there were whole communities of people, and they made it their mission. This is something that we can do.

Imperialism is the enemy of humanity. The Vietnam War is horrible, and this is something we can do. We have a 9-to-5 job. We have a regular life, but this is something that we can do, and we can do it together, and we can bond. And that's beautiful.

What Sam Marcy would tell his followers is that the community that built those puppets, that's a thousand times more valuable than some kid who thinks he's Lenin. A community like that has longevity. People are doing that their whole life, and they're taking on a contribution.

If you've been doing this as long as I have you realize there are some people who come around and they see that they don't get the immediate result that they want; They see that they don't fulfill their dictator fantasy that they have; They see that this isn't the best way to deal with their parental issues or whatever, and then they go away. For a year they know more than everybody. No one knows anything better then they do. They can debate everybody, but then, after just a short time of intense activism, they're gone.

But those people who came together to build the puppets and build community around it and learn to work together, they keep going. And generation after generation, year after year, they build those puppets. And that is what we need to build with the Center for Political Innovation. We need a network of people who are committed to opposing imperialism, who learn to trust each other and rely on each other, and carry out operations, build some beautiful puppets, some beautiful artwork, put on beautiful conferences, and keep this movement alive! We need a network of people who love each other and trust each other and can work together and can serve the purpose of representing the anti-imperialist movement in America. That is what we need, and that is what I want us to build with the Center for Political Innovation.

I remember the first time I went to a big anti-war rally, and it was in New York City. I'd never been to New York City. I was 18 years old. Me and my high school buddy, we went up to Cleveland, and we got on a bus from the American Friends Service Committee, the Quakers, and we went to New York City. It was in April of 2006, and it was one of the last anti-war marches before Obama took office, in the last years of the Bush Administration. The Democrats were mobilizing people to march against the war in those days, and this was a huge anti-war rally. My friend and I, we were just in awe. I'd never been to New York City, and I'm looking up at the skyscrapers. I'm seeing this communist group over here and this other communist group over here. As we got towards the end of the march, I'll never forget—I will never, never forget—there was a group of old men in wheelchairs on the side of the march. Not a big group, probably only five or six of them, if that. They had a big banner. You know what it said? "Veterans of the Abraham Lincoln Brigade Against the War in Iraq."

Now, in my history of the Communist Party, I quote from Angelo Heron's autobiography. He wrote a book called *You Cannot Kill the Working Class* and in that book, he talks about being a Black organizer in the US South, about how the Communist Party dealt with the racism that was deeply entrenched in the communities. He wrote:

> "I remember especially one white worker, a carpenter, who was one of the first people I talked to in Atlanta. He was very friendly to me. He came to me one day and said that he agreed with the program, but something was holding him back from joining the Unemployment Council.

> "What's that, Jim?" I asked. Really, though, I didn't have to ask. I knew the South, and I could guess. "Well, I just don't figure that white folks and Negroes should mix together," he said. "It won't never do to organize them in one body."

> I said: "Look here, Jim. You know that the carpenters and all the other workers get a darn sight less pay for the same work in the South than they do in other parts. Did you ever figure out why?"

> He hadn't.

> "Well," I said, "I'll tell you why. It's because the bosses have got us all split up down here. We Southern workers are as good fighters as there are anywhere, and yet we haven't been able to get equal wages with the workers in other places, and we haven't got any rights to speak of. That's because we've been divided. When the whites go

out on strike, the bosses call in the Negroes to scab. When the Negroes strike, the bosses call in the whites to scab.

"Did you ever figure out why the unions here are so weak? It's because the whites don't want to organize with the Negroes, and the Negroes don't trust the whites.

"We haven't got the simplest human rights down here. We're not allowed to organize and we're not allowed to hold our meetings except in secret. We can't vote— most of us— because the bosses are so anxious to keep the Negroes from voting that they make laws that take this right away from the white workers too.

"We Southern workers are like a house that's divided against itself. We're like an army that goes out to fight the enemy and stops on the way because its men are all fighting each other.

"Take this relief business, now," I said. "The commissioners tell the whites that they can't give them any more relief because they have to feed so many Negroes, and the Negroes ought to be chased back to the farms. Then they turn around and tell the Negroes that us off, and get us scrapping with each other.

"Now suppose the white unemployed, and the Negro unemployed, all go to the commissioners together and say: 'We're all starving. We're all in need. We've decided to get together into one strong, powerful organization to make you come across with relief.'

"Don't you think that'll bring results, Jim?" I asked him. "Don't you see how foolish it is to go into the fight with half an army when we could have a whole one? Don't you think that an empty belly is a pretty punk exchange for the honor of being called a 'superior' race? And can't you realize that as long as one foot is chained to the ground the other can't travel very far?"

Jim didn't say anything more that day. I guess he went home and thought it over. He came back about a week later and invited me to his house. It was the first time he'd ever had a Negro in the house as a friend and equal. When I got there I found two other Negro workers that Jim had brought into the Unemployment Council.

About a month later Jim beat up a rent collector who was boarding up the house of an evicted Negro worker. Then he went to work and organized a committee of whites and Negroes to see the mayor about the case. "Today it's the black worker across town; tomorrow it'll be me,"

Jim told the mayor." There are a lot of Jims today, all over the South."

That was the Communist Party's approach to racism. Completely opposite of the "woke" "white privilege" stuff. All these people who talk about "class reductionism! class reductionism!" don't know what the hell they're talking about. The picket line and class solidarity has been the most effective battering ram against racial division. The woke academics, funded by Wall Street foundations have rewritten the history of the anti-racist struggle to ignore all of that beautiful history of working people coming together. We have the tough job of putting forward the line that built the tenant unions of the South, the sharecroppers unions, the textile unions, that built the labor movement. This kind of class solidarity, putting the needs of the oppressed first so that the whole class can advance. That was the line that created industrial unions in this country.

Communists around the world have deep roots in communities. They don't here in the United States. I always tell people if you want to study the history of American communism, there's two groups you can study: one, the Communist Party before World War II, before McCarthyism, in the 1930s when they were big, when they were with Roosevelt… and you can study the Black Panthers in the 1970s. They had deep roots in the community. Everybody else, well, they haven't really accomplished much. You maybe you can go back to Eugene Debs or the IWW or the folks that that came before the Russian Revolution, but but post-1917, there's really only two groups in American history that had significant impact on society. One group might have done something here or something there, but but really, those are the only two groups that ever have deep roots among the masses of the American people.

But when I go to global communist youth gatherings, I see parties that have millions of members, that have deep roots in communities. I have told this story before, and I'm going to tell it again because there might be somebody here tonight who hasn't heard it, so I'm going to tell it again. The first time I ever went to a World Festival of Youth and Students, the global communist youth festival was in 2013. I went to Quito, Ecuador, and our plane landed in Ecuador, and I was with five communists from the United States. And we're there, and they moved us to a special section of the airport where

Around the world, Communist parties have deep roots in communities and neighborhoods.

the different communist groups from around the world that were there for the festival were gathering. They had buses that were picking us up taking us to the festival. We're all there sitting in the airport, we're trading newspapers, you know, the communists from Vietnam are over here, the communists from Angola are over here, the communists from Sri Lanka are over here, the Venezuelans and the Vietnamese are over here, we're talking with each other.

Then the airport starts to get quiet. Gets quiet for a minute, people start whispering that the plane from North Korea has just arrived, and then the whole airport goes silent. And a door flies open, bam, and they march in, in perfect unison. And the men are wearing suits and ties, and the women are wearing traditional Korean gowns, and they march in, in perfect unison. That whole airport is dead silent.

Then one person starts clapping, and then another person starts clapping, and then pretty soon I was standing in an airport with thousands of communists who were on their feet cheering for the Kim Il Sung Youth of North Korea. And in that moment, tears poured down my face, and I thought about all the Korean people who have died at the hands of our government, and I thought about how I am an anti-imperialist in every ounce of my being, and this is where I belong. That was a great moment in my life. I will never forget.

I am so happy that we have been selected to attend the World Youth Festival in Russia in 2024. And I'm really happy to have Chris Helali on the National Preparatory Committee working on it with us.

We are prepared to have a press conference sponsored by the Russian Mission to the United Nations, making clear we have the absolute legal right to participate in the festival. We have to be vocal about this. What they doing to the Uhuru movement right now should be on the front page of every newspaper. If they can convict Chairman Omali, Penny Hess, and Jesse Nevele, then they have pretty much declared it illegal to be an anti-imperialist activist.

Another thing I will never forget from World Festival of Youth and Students in 2013 was talking to Communists from Japan. I learned that Communists in Japan don't talk about Hiroshima and Nagasaki the way Communists around the world do, because they don't want to play into the talking points of the hard line militarist right-wing in Japan that often invokes the atomic bombs, and tries to ignore the horrendous crimes of Japanese imperialism against the Chinese and Korean people. In fact, a very high percentage of those who died in the atomic blasts were Korean slave laborers, dragged to Japan to work in war industries with no pay.

In fact, I learned that the majority of the Japanese Communist Party prior to the Second World War had been Koreans. And that one of the main things they did was sabotage the armaments they manufactured. They worked to make sure the bombs and shells that were fired wouldn't detonate. They worked to make sure some of the torpedoes that were fired from Japanese submarines at US ships didn't explode… and that reminded me of my grandfather and his ship in the pacific. Come to think of it, there's a good chance I might not be standing here today if it wasn't for some Korean Communists! Its wild to think about. [Applause]

We Love Our Country

Realizations like that and weird coincidences like that with Carl Geiser over the years have gotten me to realize there's a reason I'm doing this. I'm here for a reason. I'm doing this because I think God put me on this Earth for a reason. I'm here serving a purpose.

And you know, I have—I mean, we can tell the stories, but you know why all those people on the painting are so great and so remembered? It's because of what they did, what they accomplished in the real world. Fred Hampton built a free breakfast program. He organized the people of Chicago into a Rainbow Coalition, and for that, he was such a threat to the American status quo that he was murdered. Huey Long, the leader in Louisiana, who Huey Newton, the founder of the Black Panthers, is named after, said "every man a king." He built roads and highways all over the state. He was so loved for the programs that he provided. He built the Share Our Wealth movement all over the country. William Z. Foster, the leader of the American Communist Party, who organized an organization with unemployment councils and trade unions and was an amazing dynamic leader writer— you know, I always encourage people to study his works— but he was a brilliant trade unionist and organizer. Anna

Louise Strong, I just read you her beautiful work. They're all great because of what they did. They're not great because somebody came along and gave them a title. They're not great because somebody came along and put a crown upon their head and said, "You are the one." That's not how it works.

I keep meeting older folks, people who have been doing this for a long time, that know that it's time for somebody to step up to the plate. Right when AOC got into office—remember that? I remember when AOC got in there, and you know, I met so many older folks who went on delegations to Cuba and went on delegations to Nicaragua, and they tried so hard to like AOC. They wanted to like AOC. She's young, she's good-looking, and she says she's a socialist, but maybe she can be good. Well, she wasn't good, was she? But they tried. They wanted there to be somebody that they could believe in.

And look, I have to say this, and it's not what people like to hear, and I've heard a million excuses from people about why it's not the case, but you just have to acknowledge it. People who've been waiting for years for a real socialist movement that is really trying new ideas and really expanding and really building deep roots among the community and really aiming high and not just in the same old hamster wheel of doing the same old thing… those folks shouldn't be waiting any longer, because that organization is right here in this room!
[Applause]

We are the ones you've been waiting for. This organization is what you've been looking for, and you can make so many excuses about why we're not it. I'm sure that we're all not the right kind of LGBTQXYZ, we're the wrong nationality, we're from the wrong part of the country, we use the wrong words, whatever… but you cannot deny that we are here and we are doing it and we're getting better at it! They have thrown everything they can at us to make us stop! And if we were going to stop, we would have stopped by now. And if we were a fraud, if we were one of their plants, they'd be making it a hell of a lot easier for us, wouldn't they? They've thrown everything they can at us, but we keep coming back, and we have proved that we won't back down, we won't go away, we won't fade away. We are what people have been waiting for, and it's time that folks came forward and just recognized us for what we are. Maybe we don't sound the way you thought we would sound. Maybe we don't look the way they thought we would look, but you cannot deny that we are here. [Applause]

The reason that we're the ones cut out for this task is because we love our country. And there are some people, when we talk about patriotic socialism, they get kind of a clever look in their eye and they're like, "Oh, people think socialism is anti-American, so you're going to be the patriotic socialist. I get it." No! We actually love this country. We don't love the government, we don't love the big banks and corporations, but we actually love this country. We love the people of this country. We love the optimistic glow of hope that flows through this society. We love the fact that people have come here from all over the world in all kinds of different circumstances—some people dragged here in chains, some people jumping over fences; There's people from all over the world, different corners of this planet, that have all been dragged to one spot by the imperialist system.

We've come here because we have a will to survive. Why are there so many amazing Black musicians and Black athletes? Well, think about what the Black community has been subjected to—genocidal conditions, the transatlantic slave trade, millions of people slaughtered. You think about the death camp they had in Angola, Louisiana, where they were working people to death. And the reason that the Black community in America, the reason people like Michael Jordan are known all over the planet, the reason that Jazz and R&B is listened to all across this planet—that's because there's a beauty in the American Black community, because it represents those who had this amazing, unbeatable will to survive. They survived all of that horror. This is a strong people.

And you think about other nationalities that have come here. People have come to this country because they want to build, they want to grow, they believe that their kids could have a better life, and they go through all kinds of hardship in order to get onto these shores from different corners of the planet, all because they want to grow, they want to build, they want to construct. And now we're all gathered here— white, black, Arab, Asian, Latino—we're all here gathered in this one little tract of land between the Atlantic and the Pacific. And now the imperialists are telling us, "Well, we gotta accept being poor in order to save our system. You've all just gotta be poor, so you know that American Dream thing? Turn that off, turn that off, and just accept being poor. It's for the environment, it's for CO2, whatever. Just accept being poor. Look at your phone and be dazzled." And they think this is going to work.

It's only a matter of time before the US imperialists realize that they have been the stupidest imperialists in history. What they've done is they've gathered millions of people from all over the planet, millions of the strongest, boldest, most fearless people… and they dragged them all into one place so that we can all come together and kick their ass! [Applause followed by chants of "We are City Builders! We are City Builders!]

Revolution is Self-Defense

I want to clarify another point, which is the issue of a peaceful transition to socialism. Many of our comrades internationally feel they must emphasize that they don't think it is possible. This makes sense in a certain historical context. When Mao was facing off with Khrushchev revisionism amid the Sino-Soviet split, part of that was Khrushchev insisting on a peaceful transition to socialism. Khrushchev told people in Africa and Asia and Latin America that they couldn't pick up a gun for their national liberation. When Khrushchev came in after the death of Stalin, he said, "Well, America has the atomic bomb, so all you people around the world that are fighting for your freedom can't do it. It's too dangerous." And he tried to call off the world revolution in the name of the USA having the atomic bomb.

Well, Mao said, "No, no, we're not going to accept that." And Mao was very critical of Khrushchev and his statement about a peaceful transition to socialism. And you know, it's not that we disagree. Its a matter of emphasis.

Its one thing to say that to say that a peaceful transition to socialism is unlikely because the capitalists don't really believe in their democratic ideals and that as the people organize they will respond by setting up a fascist state and they will repress people. The people will have to defend themselves. Saying that is one thing.

That's very different than saying that you advocate a violent revolution. We need to be clear on this. This is nuance. Nuance is something that people on the internet don't seem to be able to handle, but I know you all can handle because this is in real life. Is it possible that we could have a situation in the United States where our ability to peacefully organize is suppressed, where democracy is turned off, where we'll be forced to do what Abraham Lincoln did and defend our democratic rights and carry out a social revolution? Is that possible? And would that involve violence? That's possible, sure. But we don't want that, and we don't advocate that. We advocate a peaceful transition to socialism. The question is, will they allow it?

If a violent revolution happens, it doesn't come from us. We want a peaceful transition. It comes from them and their refusal to allow it. John F. Kennedy said, "Those who make peaceful revolution impossible make violent revolution inevitable." And we have to be clear about this, and this is important in our particular context. And the reason that it's important in our particular context is not simply because of this nuance. It's not simply a legal question either.

Working-class people, right now, are having chaos brought into their communities by this system. The ruling elite are fighting with each other. There's all this fear of civil war. And what working people want is stability. And if we approach them saying that what we want is civil war, what we want is violence, what we want is chaos, we're looking like we're on the wrong side. We want an end to the chaos. We want an end to the violence. We want an end to the instability. We want to bring order to the United States of America. And our four-point plan that we've written out, that is much like the Bolsheviks—what did they offer? Did they offer chaos and violence? No, they offered peace, land, and bread. And that is what our four-point plan is: economic programs, policies that would change the nature of US society, that would empower the working class, that would weaken the power of the capitalist. That is what we advocate.

If those four points were implemented, that would be a huge push on the road to socialism and emboldening the working class. And we advocate that this program, those four points, as a way of bringing stability. However, I've always pointed out that all the great communist revolutions of history, they're not made by communists going around and advocating violence. They're acts of self-defense. And nothing is more American than the right to self-defense. [Applause]

This is what Henry Wallace said during the Second World War. He said, "The people's revolution aims at peace, not at violence. But if the rights of the common man are attacked, it unleashes the ferocity of the she-bear who has lost a cub. When Nazi psychologists tell their master Hitler that we in the United States may be able to produce hundreds of thousands of planes but that we have no will to fight, they are only fooling themselves and fooling him. The truth is that when the rights of the American people are transgressed, as they have been transgressed, the American people will fight with a relentless fury. They will drive the ancient tonic gods back into their caves. The gotterdammerung is coming for Odin and his crew. The people are on the march toward an even fuller freedom than even the most fortunate peoples of the world have hitherto enjoyed. The people's revolution is on the march, and the devil and all his angels cannot prevail against her."

I'm going to end with this. You can join CPI, you can not join CPI, you can get involved in the work that this organization is doing, or you can choose not to, but this train is heading out of the station. So it's time to get on board, because where we are headed **NO ONE KNOWS WHERE**.

Thank you very much.

www.ingramcontent.com/pod-product-compliance
Lightning Source LLC
Chambersburg PA
CBHW061300250726
48653CB00002B/696